A Simple Road Map to Publish Your Book

ALICE BRIGGS

Indie Route 101
A Simple Road Map to Publish Your Book

Copyright © 2020 by Alice Briggs

All rights reserved. No part of this book may be reproduced or transmitted in any form or by any means without written permission of the author.

ISBN: 978-1-948666-25-1

Published by:
Alice Arlene Ltd Co Press
Lubbock, TX

Dedicated to all those who go on the adventure of indie publishing, may your journey be delightful and informative.

And to my friends and family who support me in all that I do. I appreciate all of you more than you will ever know.

Contents

1. Quick Start Map 1
2. Why Indie? 5
3. KU vs Wide 11
4. Text vs Image 19
5. Research 23
6. Editing 27
7. Formatting 31
8. Cover Design 35
9. Meta Data 49
10. Publish 51
11. Marketing 55

Resources 57

Author Note 59

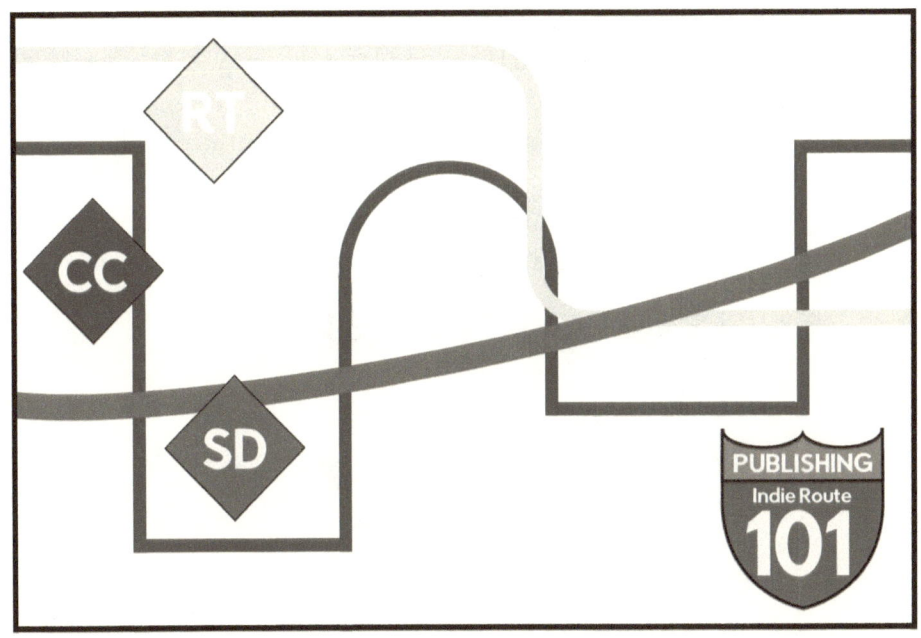

CHAPTER ZERO

Quick Start Map

THOUGH BRIEF, THIS book still covers a lot of ground. I'm giving you publishing ideas, no matter where you are in your journey. Publishing has a lot of moving pieces, so you can easily bite off too much at once. The biggest reason for this is that new authors try and do everything all at once. Please don't do this!

None of the steps are extraordinarily difficult although they each require work. Many authors publish every day, so these steps are definitely doable. I recommend that you choose your desired course of action and take one step at a time until you have completed that step. Then take the next step. This will help you so that you don't become stressed out and keep you moving toward your goal of holding your finished, published book in your hand.

Feel free to read through the entire book, but please don't become overwhelmed. You can do this! Authors just like you do so every day.

Choose your publishing adventure!

The Sunday Drive: This is perfect for new authors publishing their first book. I recommend you start with Kindle Unlimited and a text-based book (see p. 20). Watch for this symbol throughout the book.
1. Choose your format: Kindle Select eBook - p. 12
2. Edit - p. 27
3. Formatting: Done for you, ePub only - p. 32
4. Premade cover design: JPG - p. 39
5. Metadata - p. 49
6. Upload to KDP for Kindle Unlimited - p. 51

Quick Start Map

The Road Trip: This is perfect for a published author who wants to expand their reach or a new author who is willing to take a few more steps before they publish their book. I recommend you add a print version of your book through KDP. You may also be a children's book author with an image-based book (see p. 21). Watch for this symbol throughout the book.

1. Choose your format: KDP Print - 14
2. Edit - p. 27
2. Formatting: Done for you, ePub and PDF - p. 32
3. Custom cover design: JPG and PDF - p. 41, 44
4. Metadata - p. 49
5. Upload to KDP - p. 51

The Cross Country: This is the most complex journey. You can choose which pieces you want to do and when you want to do them. You don't have to do them all at once. Avoid overwhelm by choosing an additional piece and adding it as you're able. Watch for this symbol throughout the book.

1. Choose your formats: ebook, print, and audio - pgs. 15-17
2. Edit - p. 27
2. Formatting: Self, ePub, and PDF - p. 33
3. Custom cover design: JPG, and PDF for KDP and Ingram Spark (IS) - p. 41, 44
4. Metadata - p. 49
5. Deselect Kindle Select if you selected it previously
6. Upload to additional providers - 51
7. Ask Ingram Spark to transfer your title from KDP - p. 15, 52

CHAPTER ONE

Why Indie?

AS YOU ENTER the publishing realm, you'll encounter entirely new vocabulary, which can be very confusing. I'll start by defining a few terms to clarify I mean in the pages that follow.

Traditional publishing means that an agent represents you and submits your book to a publisher. If accepted, they pay you an advance and take the rights to your book. An advance is pre-payment against the royalties they expect the book to earn. So you need to earn out that advance before you receive any more money. You typically split any royalties or advances with your agent. The barrier to entry here is very high, and the time frame for publication can take from nine to twenty-four months.¹

Vanity publishing is a predatory outfit that acts as your publisher at great expense to you. You pay them; they do not pay you, and they often also require you to sign over the rights to your book. They may also provide you with very expensive but poor-quality services, such as editing and cover design. You may also have to purchase large quantities of your book at exorbitant prices.

A **Full service author services company** will provide you with a variety of in-house services to prepare your manuscript for publication. Prices and quality of services vary. This type of publishing overlaps somewhat with vanity publishers, so buyer beware, but legitimate companies will do a good job for you and your book.

Indie or independent publishing is when you act as the general contractor for your book. You remain in full control of the process and hire people to do parts of the process that you can't or don't want to do for yourself.

Self-publishing has become nearly a meaningless term, as most of the above, except traditional publishers, will refer to themselves as self-publishers. I define self-publishing as someone who does every step themselves. Very few people can effectively handle all aspects of their publishing journey, but this can be a viable place to start. You can then hire professionals as you are able. Downsides exist for this, especially with covers and editing, but people have bootstrapped their books and then upgraded elements later when they could.

I am proudly indie, but this book won't dictate what you should do or how you should do it. The following are some factors to consider as you determined which path to choose.

---

1 Robert Lee Brewer, "How Long Does It Take to Get a Book Published?" Writer's Digest, June 9, 2020, https://www.writersdigest.com/getting-published/how-long-does-it-take-to-get-a-book-published.

Accessibility

With traditional publishing, you are at the mercy of finding an agent to read, accept, and sell your book. Not all publishers accept all genres. Publishing has traditionally been a tightly controlled industry with formidable gatekeepers.

Vanity publishers have been around for many years. They are so named because they appeal to your vanity—a published title regardless of merit in exchange for a large sum of money. Many have pivoted and call themselves self-publishers. And here is where the labels become very murky.

Some full-service companies offer an out-of-the-box publishing services and do a decent job for authors for a reasonable fee. But others charge exorbitant prices for inferior work.

Publishing is now accessible to all, and that is a fabulous opportunity, but it also creates a buyer-beware environment for those who want a quick fix.

Quality

A common misconception is that self-published books are inferior in quality to traditionally published titles. And that's a fair assessment from many, to be sure.

However, when you are fully indie, you can have your book polished to the highest standard. You can also continuously improve the quality of your work. You can fix typos and upload revised files, and there will be typos, even in traditionally published books.

You can absolutely produce a product that meets or exceeds the quality of traditionally published titles.

Speed

Unquestionably, indie publishing is a much faster process than traditional publishing. The fastest you can hope to have a traditionally published title available for purchase by your readers is around nine to twelve months. Some indie-published authors manage to publish in that many days. Granted, that's faster than most, and they may have streamlined their process over time, but it's not unheard of. You can even publish that fast to a high standard if you plan ahead and write quickly.

Agility

Agility relates to and depends on speed. But aside from initial publishing, you can also change and revise parts of your book, such as your blurb and covers as trends change or as you learn more about what your readers want. Changes for most of these things are as simple as copying and pasting new text onto your dashboards. Test and measure what is more effective if you desire.

Also, when it comes to quality, you can correct typos as you find them or a few times a year, whatever you like. And soon, your book is perfect!

Control

I've touched some on this above, but I feel that it warrants its own section. When you go indie, you are the contractor of the building that is your book. You are free to DIY or hire professionals, depending on your desires and capabilities. You are also free to decide where to publish and distribute your book, which I'll address more in the next chapter.

And if you make an error, you are free to readjust and continue on better than before.

Retention of Intellectual Property Rights

When you create something, you are the copyright owner of your creation with few exceptions, such as work for hire. Copyright, at least in the United States, lasts for seventy-five years after your death. When you publish, consider the long-term implications of what you're doing, not just for yourself, but also for your heirs for a couple of generations.

Keeping the rights of your work also means that you can do many things with it. Depending on the type of book you're producing, you can license the rights for audio, merchandise, and film. Or you can handle some of those things yourself.

Royalties

Traditionally published authors receive around 10–15 percent of the purchase price in royalties, and they may have to split that with their agents. Depending on where you publish or distribute, you can earn as much as 85 percent in royalties as an indie author.

Marketing

For me, the major benefit of being a traditionally published author would have been someone to market for me. And while that does happen for a few big-name authors, for the vast majority, a traditional publisher won't even consider someone without an existing platform or the capability to have a built-in market.

Backlist

Your backlist is all your previously published titles. Traditional publishers mostly—if not entirely—ignore this mine of potential revenue. They promote new releases, but have you ever seen an ad for a book that's been out for a couple of years? Probably not. Yet, if you've signed over your rights to your IP, then all of that work just sits. Whereas, if you still have the rights to your book, you can also encourage readers to find your backlist titles, and hopefully they will read everything you've written so far. If your profit from a book is five dollars and you only promote your most recent title, then you'll earn five dollars for each reader who finds you. But if you have a backlist of ten titles and the reader goes back and reads them all, you've now earned an additional fifty dollars from that reader.

You also can promote books in your backlist that relate to current events. Imagine if you had published a book on surviving pandemics in 2015. When March 2020 hit, you ran a few ads to that book. It probably would have sold very well.

CHAPTER TWO

KU vs Wide

INDIE AUTHORS CHOOSE one of two paths for publishing: exclusive with KDP in KU or what they call "wide," meaning world-wide through other distributors. This is for e-books, as the exclusivity requirements for KDP's Kindle Select or Kindle Unlimited apply to e-books only. Both are viable options, and authors can make a lot of money with both. Choose the one that fits with what you want and that best fits your marketing strategy.

I was in KU for the first few years of my publishing career and then went wide. I've heard of others who are wide and then go into KU, and still others have a hybrid approach, so you are not making a permanent decision. Do be aware that many readers are only KU or on other platforms, and others do both, so if you are marketing to KU readers, they may not follow you wide and vice versa.

Kindle Direct Publishing

KDP has revolutionized the publishing industry. Prior to Amazon's KDP, you could indie publish in a few ways, but Amazon provided a means to connect the potential reader with the indie author through the Kindle. This remains the single most popular platform for readers and authors, at least in the US, which is a massive market. It is also one of the easiest platforms to use.

It's important to note that although you've written one book, you have at least two products if you do both an e-book and print. The distributors treat them separately, though they are linked on your dashboard and on the product pages that the reader sees.

Ebook

Your e-book is more like a webpage than a book in function. You can upload a mobi file, which is Amazon's proprietary format, or an ePub, which other e-book retailers accept as well.

You can choose between a 35 percent and a 70 percent royalty rate, which is not as simple as it sounds. The 70 percent royalty rate comes with some restrictions. Your price must be between $2.99 and $9.99, the list price of the print book must be at least 20 percent more than the e-book, and it must be available in all geographies for which you have rights. This usually means all, unless you've sold or given those rights to someone else. They will also charge you a delivery fee, which can be significant if you have a lot of images. You will need to do the math to see which percentage makes the most economic sense for your book. Amazon has a calculator that does the math for you as you upload your book. This is my preferred method.

If you are not also in Kindle Select, you will not be eligible for the 70 percent royalty for sales in Brazil, Japan, Mexico, and India. Your royalty rate in those countries will be 35 percent. You should consider this if those are your primary markets.

There are a few requirements for books in the 35 percent royalty rate. The maximum price is $200, and the minimum depends on the size of the file delivered. Link to details in the footnotes.[2]

Kindle Select is the author facing name of Kindle Unlimited, the exclusive subscription available through Amazon. For a monthly fee, readers can read any title enrolled in the program for "free". KDP pays authors based on the number of pages read. They calculate payment in some mysterious way that changes and announce the new rate each month. Over the last four years, this payment has ranged from $.004 to $.0053.

If you enroll in Kindle Select, you can have a maximum of 10 percent of the material available digitally in any other form anywhere else. This does not include print or audio. You can have print and audio versions of your book available outside of Amazon, but not the ebook. You can have a short exerpt of your book on your website, for example, but typically not 2-3 chapters.

---

[2] https://kdp.amazon.com/en_US/help/topic/G200634560.

Print

KDP Print is the print-on-demand arm of Amazon's indie author platform. This was formerly called Create Space, which merged with KDP Print in 2018. You now have one dashboard for both e-book and print, and the function is largely the same.

Print on demand (POD) means that KDP prints your book only if and when someone purchases it. This could be you purchasing author copies or a reader purchasing on Amazon. This differs from the traditional method of printing hundreds or thousands of copies, storing them, and shipping them to bookstores. Because of the nature of the process, POD tends to have a larger tolerance or wiggle room to allow for your design. Traditional off-set printing is more accurate, but the tradeoff is a large upfront expense and boxes of books stashed in the garage or under the bed. Some authors do sell enough on their own to do offset printings of their books, so this isn't a complete either/or choice as long as you have your own ISBN. (See Chapter 8 for more information on ISBNs.)

Paperback is the only format available through KDP Print, currently, although additional formats are rumored to be in beta at the time of this writing. Royalties for books sold on Amazon marketplaces are 60 percent less the cost to print the book. Royalties for expanded distribution are 40 percent less the cost to print the book. When you upload your book, KDP has calculators that will show you what your royalty will be in the various areas. I also recommend that you research expected prices within your genre and categories, but we'll discuss that in a later chapter.

KDP offers quite a wide range of trim sizes, the term that refers to the width and height of the book. You can find all of them at the link in the endnotes.³

Ingram Spark

Ingram Spark (IS) is the indie author branch of Lightning Source, an international company that has been serving the publishing industry for fifty years. By printing through IS, an indie author can access the same distribution network as traditional publishers. IS also provides the ability to do hardcover books by POD.

With a similar process to KDP's, IS is often the next step for new authors after KDP. If you are planning on adding IS in the future, I recommend choosing a trim size that you can use in both places. Many, but not all, are the same on both platforms.

IS is not recommended for e-books, although they offer that as an option. Their expertise and platform are best for print books.

If you first publish with KDP and then wish to add IS, open an account with IS and then ask them to transfer your title. They will assist you in the current process. Currently it consists of filling out a form, and then they import all your files. Do not create a title for the book, they will do so for you.

---

3   https://kdp.amazon.com/en_US/help/topic/G201834180.

Going Wide with eBooks

Distributors

You can go with multiple places for wide distribution of your books. You can target many world-wide marketplaces through aggregators such as Draft2Digital, Publish Drive, Streetlib, and Smashwords. You can go directly to Google Play, Barnes & Noble, Apple, and Kobo. These are the four largest marketplaces outside of Amazon as of this writing. The markets the aggregators serve change, so I won't go into that here. You'll want to research current agreements and information when you're ready to make that decision.

You'll want to consider how many places you want to upload to. If you choose many, I recommend using some kind of form or check sheet so that you can keep the places organized. I adapted the Upload Check Sheet on page 54 from what I used for a recent series.

If you are not going direct, then the aggregator will take a cut of the royalties you receive from the platforms where they push your book. You may prefer that slight cut to uploading manually yourself to many places.

All of these platforms will allow preorders except for KDP print. If you're doing a preorder, then you will need to go back and upload your KDP print files once the book is live.

I do not use Draft2Digital, because when I went wide, PublishDrive distributed everywhere they do plus many others. However, PD has changed how they pay their royalties, so I would encourage you to go with D2D instead as PD is no longer user-friendly for beginner authors.

Also, when I went wide, Google Play was difficult to manage direct as was Apple. I understand this has changed recently, but I have not pulled my books from PD to go direct as of yet. I'll probably do that shortly. Although you can change later, part of my problem is the number of books that I have written—nearly thirty!—that I must move, so it takes more time now than if I had started there.

Most people first use D2D when going wide. You'll hit all the major retailers that way, and they're a great company to work with from all I've heard.

Audio

The audio book format is growing in popularity among readers and profitability for authors. Amazon also has an exclusive platform that you can go through, or you can release on other platforms without exclusivity contracts.

Audio is on my list of things to do, but I haven't released audiobooks yet, so I will leave this subject to those with more experience than I. I recommend Audio for Authors by Bradley Charbonneau[4] and Audio for Authors by Joanna Penn[5] - links in the endnotes.

---

4   Audio for Authors by Bradley Charbonneau: https://books2read.com/u/bzg5Jq
5   Audio for Authors by Joanna Penn: https://books2read.com/u/4A7ZGo

CHAPTER THREE

Text vs Image

Text based books

Text-based books are just like what the phrase says: nearly all text with few if any images. Genres include most fiction from middle grade on up and nonfiction with few charts, images, etc. If you have a text-based book, skip to the next chapter for research. If you have some images in your book, the information in the image-based section will apply to you.

Text vs Image

Image based books

Image-based books include children's picture books, cookbooks, and art books. I would also include nonfiction that relies heavily on charts, graphs, screenshots, or other image-based content.

In the next section, you'll do some research on specifics for your categories and hopefully decide which trim size is best for what you want to do. Right now, I want you to understand a bit why that decision is especially important if you are including images in your books.

I'll review some terms and their meanings. Bleed is an extra amount outside of the trim size of the book. It is used when you want the image to go to the edge of the page. It is typically 0.125" on all sides except the interior edge or margin where the book is bound, otherwise known as the gutter. This allows for any slight errors in printing so you don't have a white line on the edge of your page.

In order for an image to print well, it needs to be 300 ppi or pixels per inch. This means that the image must be 300 pixels for every inch that the image will be in the book. You will need to include the bleed in that amount. For example, my children's books are 8x10, so the size of the image needs to be 8.125 x 10.25. (8 + bleed) x (10 + bleed twice). You can then multiply those numbers by 300 to get 2438 x 3075 pixels. This is a minimum number. As you can see, the trim size plays a critical role here.

If you are commissioning artwork, I recommend giving the illustrator a slightly larger format to work from, such as 9x11 for an 8x10 book, but let them know they should not put anything important on the outside one inch or so. They will have more flexibility when formatting your book so that you have a sufficiently large image.

If the illustrator is working analog and plans to scan in the work or if you are using scans or images of your artwork or of other photographs, including screenshots, you will want to ensure that the resulting jpg images are at least 300 ppi at the size you want to use them. I prefer starting from larger and going to smaller, and then I compress the images when exporting the final files.

Also note, that for POD, any color means that your book will be in full color for printing purposes. This increases the cost of production, which is passed on to you. There is no such thing as spot color in POD—it's all or nothing. So full-spread images will cost the same as small color changes in text. In my opinion, go big or go home with the color as long as you do it tastefully.

Research Rest Area

CHAPTER FOUR

Research

I HAVE A PRE-TRIP Preparation PDF at the end of this chapter that you can use to collect the information I discuss below when you do your research. Use whatever will be easy for you to refer back to later. I also suggest you grab the Marketing PDF. I'm not going to go into marketing in this book as I still have too much to learn about that. But what I do know is that much of the same research that you will find helpful in publishing your book will be useful to you when you market. I wish I had known this sooner.

I want you to do your research based on the categories you plan to use for your book. Do note that the categories are not necessarily the same for e-book and print for some genres, so make a note of those differences as you go along. Why should you do this? You want readers to be able to find your book. So you want your book to sit on the same shelf as similar books so that people who are interested in those books will see your book, pick it up, and hopefully fall in love. Your cover will help your book look like it fits, so make sure that the insides match the outside. Disappointed readers do not leave happy reviews, so make sure you are fulfilling your promise to your reader.

You can do research on Amazon, Goodreads, and Barnes & Noble, or perhaps Kobo if you are Canadian and expect that to be a major market for you. You don't want to spend months on this, but you want to do enough research to have a solid feel for the trends or to know that this isn't actually the right fit for your book. While disappointing, that's actually very helpful information.

Use as many of the sheets as you like, but keep each category on a separate page or pages. Write the title and subtitle of the book. Not all books have subtitles, so make a note of that. You may see trends appear. For example, punny titles are quintessentially cozy mystery. You often find long subtitles in nonfiction books. This information will help you conform to what's typical for books in your genre.

Remember, trim size is the size of the print version of the book. Even if you're not planning on doing a print version, make a note of this information in case you change your mind later. Depending on genre, print books are still popular with readers.

Book length is listed as the number of pages in the details of the book. Price is obvious. Something not so obvious is the other categories that the book may be listed in. This may give you a better idea of what categories you should use.

Also, take a screenshot of the top fifty to one hundred titles in each of your categories. This will help you understand what kind of covers people are looking for. I'll discuss that more in the cover design section, but you should address this while you're there as that will help you and save you time later.

Again, in all this, you are looking for trends. You want to know what's typical for your categories so you can better succeed in all your efforts.

A Simple Route to Publishing
Pre-Trip Preparation

Category: _____

Gather information from the bestsellers in your categories. Take screen shots of the covers of the top 100, you'll want them later.

Title: _____   Title: _____

Subtitle: _____   Subtitle: _____

Trim Size: _____   Trim Size: _____

Length: _____   Length: _____

Price: _____   Price: _____

Other Categories: Other Categories:

_____   _____

_____   _____

Title: _____   Title: _____

Subtitle: _____   Subtitle: _____

Trim Size: _____   Trim Size: _____

Length: _____   Length: _____

Price: _____   Price: _____

Other Categories: Other Categories:

_____   _____

©2020 Alice Briggs - KingdomCovers.com
Permission granted for copying for personal use only.

A Simple Route to Publishing
Marketing Research Checklist

Author	Website	Podcast	Class	FB	IG	LI	TW	Other

©2020 Alice Briggs - KingdomCovers.com
Permission granted for copying for personal use only.

CHAPTER FIVE

Editing

EDITING MAY BE the bane of most people's existence and can be the most expensive part of the publishing process. This depends on what level of editing you need and on how long your book is. I often see people asking how much it will cost to edit a book. That's like asking how long a piece of string is.

The answer is, it depends.

The most common forms of editing include developmental, line edits, and copy edits in order of comprehensiveness and expense. Proofreading is a final review of the book.

A developmental edit refers to the overall organization and structure of the book. This will vary, depending on if you're working with fiction or nonfiction. Here, you are addressing the big picture and overall content of your book. Does the book flow and make sense?

A line or copy edit are not exactly the same, but the terms are sometimes used interchangeably. Line editing includes minor rewrites and the clarification of awkward wording. Copy editing is what you typically think of when someone says "editing": the correction of grammar, typos, spelling, and punctuation.

Proofreading can happen at several points along the publishing path but comes after editing and often after formatting to catch any errors in either the words or the formatting of the book. This is right before uploading.

You will typically need to pay and/or barter for these services. Yes, bartering is alive and well in the indie sphere!

Choosing an Editor

How do you choose an editor? Ask around for recommendations. You want someone competent in your genre who knows the Chicago Manual of Style (CMoS as you'll see it often) if you are in the US. That's the acceptable style manual for published books. A retired English teacher may or may not have the skills necessary if they are not familiar with the most up-to-date CMoS rules.

Cost

The cost of editing generally depends on how much work your manuscript needs. Thus, I recommend first doing as much self and friend editing as possible. People sometimes want to skip editing due to the expense. I'll do all that I can in order to send as clean a manuscript as possible to my editor. You should especially do this if you do not choose to hire a professional editor. However, I cannot recommend a professional edit enough, but I understand if it's not possible.

How can you effectively polish your manuscript as much as possible?

Use tools, such as ProWritingAid. Grammarly is another option, but I don't recommend it as my editor and many of her colleagues avoid it. The user must be very familiar with the rules of grammar, so it might not be effective for new authors who are unsure of these rules. Spell check in your word processor is also helpful.

Ask friends or other writers in your genre to do a beta read of your book. This is often before the pro editing step, as fresh eyes will help you identify weak points in your manuscript and find many typos. The best beta readers would be in your target audience for the book, those interested in your topic or who typically read your genre.

My friend Katherine Walden wrote this book, which I also recommend: Insider Editing tips for Self-Publishers: Avoiding Embarrassing Typos and Grammatical Errors[6]. It will be an excellent resource for you.

---

[6] Insider Editing tips for Self-Publishers: Avoiding Embarrassing Typos and Grammatical Errors by Katherine Walden: https://books2read.com/u/b5kyz6

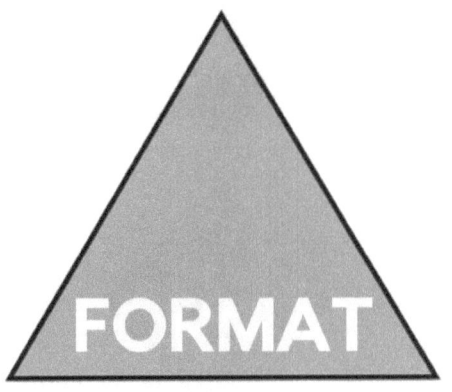

CHAPTER SIX

Formatting

E-BOOKS FUNCTION MUCH like a website does, as one continuous flow of text, unless you use a non-reflowable version. But if you've read a novel or most nonfiction on an e-reader, you've experienced the reflowable e-book. The reader can set the font and size of text among other features, so the author has less control over the final appearance of the book.

Children's books and other image-heavy books are typically in non-reflowable format. However, this can limit your readers as this format doesn't work well on all e-reader devices.

The table of contents is hyperlinked to the various chapters so you can easily navigate through the book.

EPub and mobi files are the most commonly used file formats. Mobi is KDP's proprietary file format but recently announced they would only accept EPubs. EPub is used everywhere else.

Done for you

You can hire someone to do e-book formatting, or you can use templates or online formatters, such as D2D's or Reedsy's. Scrivener will export an e-book for you. If you will be publishing multiple books, look into Vellum. It's built for Macs, but if you have a PC, you can use Mac in Cloud to run it.

If you are going with KDP and doing image-based books, Kindle Kid's Book Creator is easy to use and works well.

I use InDesign for all my formatting, which is the industry standard, but it's probably overkill for general publishing by an author.

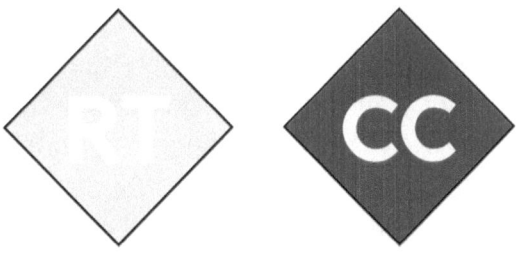

DIY

I find formatting for print a more enjoyable, though arguably more tedious task. It's the artist in me, but I love having a beautifully laid-out book. Since your book will be in print, what you choose is what it will look like in the final product.

Some terms you'll come across include:

Margin: This is probably what you think, the space around the top, outside, and bottom of your page. As I previously mentioned, the minimums for KDP are 0.25", but I recommend a larger margin, especially for the outside edge, so the reader's thumb has some space to hold the book without covering text.

Gutter: This is the space on the inside edge of the page so the left-hand side of a right-hand page and vice versa. The minimum varies based on the number of pages in your book. You can find details on this space for KDP here: https://kdp.amazon.com/en_US/help/topic/G202145400. Again, I recommend increasing those amounts to make it easy for the reader to read.

Bleed: As previously mentioned, this is typically 0.125" beyond the margins of the page. They use it for images that go to the edge. You take the image beyond the edge so that any variance in printing will not result in a white line. They trim this extra space off before they bind the book.

Trim size: This is the width and height of your book, commonly 6x9 for nonfiction books. This means that the book is 6 inches wide and 9 inches tall.

Spine width: This is the width of the spine. This depends on the number of pages and the color of the paper. Cream paper is slightly thicker than white paper, and though slight, this difference adds up quickly and will result in an error if you've used one to calculate the spine width (or downloaded a template, which I recommend) but selected the other when uploading your files.

Vellum: This is a popular way to format your books for print and e-book. D2D is developing a print formatter that is in beta stages at the time of this writing. People also format using Word or Scrivener. I use InDesign, but you might not want to deal with the fairly steep learning curve. Affinity Publisher is a comparable tool to InDesign for a one time payment.

CHAPTER SEVEN

Cover Design

A BOOK COVER CAN make or break the financial success of your book. It is the first thing that people see, and they will judge your book by its cover.

Your book cover has one purpose: to sell your book. It is the primary advertisement for what lies between the pages. It need not describe or be representational of the contents, but it should give potential readers a strong indication of what they will find inside. You want the right readers—not just any reader—to see your book. To do that, you need to meet the reader's expectations. The cover needs to be consistent with the content of the book.

Genre Consistent

People categorize and notice similarities and differences. The wise author uses this to their advantage. Look at books in your genre or any genre. Notice that they have a similar feel, similar colors, consistency in types of imagery, and similar font choices. In some genres, you see very few differences between one cover and the next.

You want to stand out from the crowd, but not too much. Your book needs to look like it fits on the shelf next to the others in your genre. This similarity tells your reader that they will most likely enjoy this book. Give the reader what they want; this leads to excellent reviews and repeat buyers.

Series Branding

If you have a series of books, you want to tighten up the similarities of your covers even more. You want people to recognize at a glance that those books belong together. You brand a series by using covers which are very similar as to imagery, fonts, and layout.

Overall Design

Your design needs to be cohesive with a clear focal point. The reader's eyes should immediately go to where you want them to focus, typically on your title or on one part of the image. Beware of trying to put too much on the cover. You have about three seconds to capture the reader's attention. Once you have their interest, you can hook them with the description and/or back cover copy. If the reader doesn't know where to look, they will scroll on by.

Check the Thumbnail

People purchase most books online in marketplaces, such as Amazon. The reader's first encounter with your book will be the cover at thumbnail size, which is almost microscopic. How your cover design holds up at the thumbnail size is an important consideration. Most successful authors and designers will tell you that your title and image must be discernible, even at thumbnail size. Some disagree as that information is right next to the image, but their opinion is in the minority.

Crowd Sourcing

Crowd-sourcing opinions on your cover can be helpful. Other eyes can spot issues you've missed. But these can also mislead you and contradict each other, especially if the commenters are not familiar with, or readers of, your genre. What appeals to a reader of sweet romance will differ from what appeals to readers of thrillers. You need to know who your readers are, which is as important as knowing what they like.

Research

Remember the screenshots you took of the best sellers in your categories? It's time to take them back out and see what trends or similarities you find. Look for colors, types of images, typefaces or fonts used, or other elements consistent across the best sellers in your genre.

Cover trends can change over time, so you might want to do this every couple of years, depending on your genre. Some genres change more quickly than others, so you should check periodically to see if you need to refresh your covers. If your sales are dipping more than you think they should, evaluate your cover. It isn't the only reason for declining sales, but it can be one of them.

In this section, I'll cover some strategies to do it yourself, although as a designer, I have to say that this rarely goes as well as I hoped. We're too close to our own work, and cover design needs a fairly comprehensive skill set. An amateur cover will negatively affect sales. But depending on your reasons for publishing, this may not matter to you.

For example, you might not worry as much about a genre-appropriate cover if you are publishing something for friends and family, if you have a platform that will buy it regardless, or if you're giving away books as gifts or for free promotion. If your name or position will sell the book, then the cover is less critical to its success. I would also add that if you are the only book or one of a few on the topic, the cover may not affect sales as much as if you have a lot of competition.

If you are marketing to a broader, more general audience, the cover will need to be on point. Although there are exceptions, this is the prevailing wisdom of many successful authors.

Interestingly, indies are leaping ahead of traditional publishing in this area. Traditional publishing relies on advertising dollars to sell books, somewhat as a brute-force attack. Many indies make much more than traditional authors, and they know that a cover that meets genre expectations will help them sell their book, so they will ensure that it does just that.

Design Basics for DIY

Both KDP and IS have templates to ensure that you get the size of the cover correct. These are based on the trim size, the number of pages, and the color of the paper that you are using. Again, while it seems like it should be insignificant, the color of the paper matters. Cream paper is slightly thicker than white and that difference adds up in a hurry. This is the number one reason for errors when uploading your book, so use your Directions for the Journey Form on page 48 and make a note of the color of paper you'll be using and stay with that.

It is best to stick with two fonts only for a book cover. Font pairing is an art form in and of itself. You can do an online search for "font pairing" and the year, and look through the results to find a pair that seems to fit your categories and the feel of your book. Be sure that the font you are choosing is available and appropriately licensed for commercial (as opposed to personal) use.

You should buy stock images from a paid site, not a free one. Free stock sites do not vet the images and leave you open to potential copyright and trademark infringements. There are many levels of copyright and potential trademark issues that you need to avoid, and the easiest way to do that is to purchase your stock through Deposit Photo, Shutterstock, or a similar site that offers some guarantee and protection to you should they mistakenly allow an image subject to copyright or trademark law. Even a brief scan of free stock sites shows many images that infringe on copyright and trademark and other image restrictions.

Cover Design

What would happen if you used an image incorrectly? It all depends, but the least troubling thing that could happen would be that you would need to take down your book and change the cover. You could be fined or sued for large sums of money. I'm not extremely risk averse, but this seems like an easily avoided hassle to just do it right the first time.

On the cover template for KDP or Ingram Spark, you'll notice that lines show where the cover will fold and safe zones. Print on demand is not as precise of a printing process as off-set printing, so they have built in those tolerances to their templates. Be aware of those as you are planning your design.

I typically use a combination of Photoshop and InDesign, but I've heard people use Canva and Gimp. From what I understand, Canva has book cover templates, but I have not used them, so I don't know how that works. Some find Affinity Photo and Affinity Designer to be good alternatives for Photoshop and Illustrator which are available for a one time fee instead of a subscription.

Two books with more helpful in-depth information are Book Cover Design Secrets by Derek Murphy[7] and The Author's Guide to Cover Design by Stuart Bache[8].

I mentioned premade covers earlier. This is an excellent starting point if budget is an issue. Many authors begin with a cover that they

---

7   Book Cover Design Secrets by Derek Murphy https://books2read.com/u/mVgEoA
8   The Author's Guide to Cover Design by Stuart Bache: https://books2read.com/u/3JXdQg

can afford and then upgrade later if they find that sales are not as strong for the book as they would like. You can change your cover whenever you wish and upload new files.

Premade covers work because of the proven principle that it is more important to nail down genre than to be a perfect description of your book. So designers can create designs that fulfill genre expectations without a specific book in mind. Many authors find these are great story starters.

Premade covers are an effective way to get a professionally designed book cover for much less. You can typically change your name, tagline, and title or any other important information on the cover without further fees. Altering the design itself may or may not be available and may come with extra fees.

Some designers are also doing what they call custom premades. These are still much less than a custom book cover, and the designer takes your information to inform their design choices. However, unlike a custom design, the resulting cover is a take-it or leave-it item once completed. When available, these are an excellent value for both the author and the designer.

If you have any questions about what is or is not allowed with either a premade or a custom premade, ask your designer before purchasing. Be aware that designers are professionals, and you are paying for their knowledge and experience, not just their time.

Cover Design

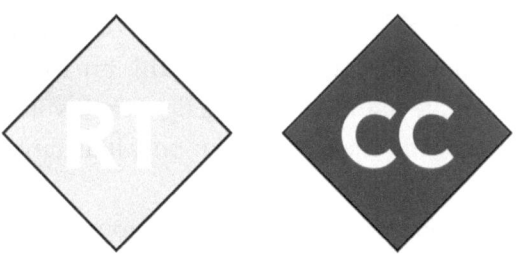

Custom

Potentially the most expensive, but arguably the best value for your time and money is a professional cover design. Ask for recommendations for designers from others in your genre/categories. Do your due diligence and look at their portfolios. A website is a sign that the person takes their business seriously and would be a point in their favor. Cover design is a booming industry and not everyone who calls themselves a designer knows what's required or is a true professional.

The designer is your partner in creating a book cover that will attract the right eyes to your book. Treat them with respect and communicate what you want before you begin and during the design process. Also remember that the designer is working to provide you with the best possible cover to help sell your book, so if they push back on your ideas or desires for changes, consider their suggestions carefully.

So where do you start? The place to start is with your book. Remember the research that you did early on with your categories? Here's another place where this research will save you lots of time and frustration. The genre or categories of your book will help you narrow down your choices for book cover designers. You can Google to find a smaller range of designers or ask for recommendations in genre-based Facebook groups. Once you've found a few who work in your genre, check out their portfolios. Do they show a strong understanding of your genre? Every artist has a style, but is the designer able to adapt to the needs of the book and author they are working with? If you see books by various authors in that designer's portfolio that look as if they are in the same series, I recommend that you go no further. The designer's job is to make your book look like you, not others. This is part of branding, and you want your unique brand, not the designer's. If your genre calls for photographic covers and the designer has only illustrations, you'll want to look elsewhere.

Once you find one with the look you're going for, then check out their terms and conditions and about pages. Do they sound like someone you could work with? Do you feel that they will get your project? Do you have common ground with the designer? You will work better with some designers than others; that's often a personality match or conflict rather than a skill level. You need to communicate well with the designer and he or she with you for the best experience possible.

Do they have information on their turnaround times and/or scheduling availability, and will that fit with your schedule? Turnaround times for a premade cover are usually quick and may be a perfect option for you, so head back to that section. Custom covers require additional time and communication back and forth. This is often reflected in the price points of those packages. Most designers work on covers in the order in which they were hired, so check with the designer on their timeframe to be sure it will fit your schedule.

In your initial communications with your chosen designer, be clear in your expectations about the process and your cover. Hopefully, the designer has made their expectations clear on their site, and yours matches them well. If you've worked with other designers, let them know what worked well and what didn't. This hopefully goes without saying, but be respectful. Your designer is a highly skilled professional and should be treated as such.

I haven't mentioned price. It probably goes without saying as this is the piece that most of us are the most acutely aware of. But price, within reason, is a secondary concern. In some ways, you get what you pay for, but in others, it's irrelevant. A $2000 sci-fi cover will not help sell your self-help book—nor would it if you spent multiples of that! It's just the wrong cover for the book.

Some designers, like myself, have various tiers of packages for design so you can choose one that best fits your book and your budget. We are your partners in this venture and want you and your book to do well. While the cover is not the only determinant of the success of your book, it is your readers' first exposure to your book.

A word of caution about sites with cheap designers and sites where the designers compete for your job. You can find some excellent designers and strong designs on such sites, but you should also be aware of potential legal risks. As the author, you will be culpable for any fines if the designer chooses images or fonts that are not licensed for commercial purposes or if they do not have the appropriate releases signed.

Information to Give to Your Designer

Your designer will need to know the following for a custom book design:
1. The genre and categories you will put your book in
2. The tone of your book
3. A synopsis of your book and any key elements. Hold these loosely, though. It is far more important that your book cover nail the genre/category than depict your exact story.
4. Samples of covers in your category(ies) that you like and why you like them. Do you like the feel, the colors, the typography, the placement of the text or other elements, the type of image, etc.? This helps your designer get a feel for what you like and what you think will work well. They may push back and make other recommendations based on their experience. Again, your designer wants your book to succeed as that's also a measure of how well they do their job. You may overrule them, but consider their points carefully before doing so.

Print

If you will be also adding print edition(s),
1. Are you doing softcover/paperback or hardcover or both?
2. What is the total number of formatted pages in your book?
3. What color paper will you be using? Nearly all uploading errors of print covers occur because the author told the designer one color and selected another when uploading the files. Amazon and IS will kick your file back because the spine size will be incorrect.
4. What do you want on the back cover as to blurb, bio, photo, etc.? Keep in mind you have a finite amount of space.
5. What is the book's trim size?

Legal Considerations

People don't usually address the legalities of a book cover, and yet if you are unaware of potential legal issues, you could find yourself in a huge mess. I am not a lawyer, and the following does not constitute legal advice—just a friendly heads up of some issues to be aware of. If you have specific questions, seek the advice of a lawyer in your area familiar with the law related to publication.

By default, the artist or designer—the same as an author—holds the copyright for their creations. Unless you have a contract that says otherwise, you do not own the cover of your book; the designer does. Neither of you would own the images within that design unless you created them. In effect, the creator of the image and the designer licenses their images to you for use on your book cover. It is generally understood that the image will also be used in promotional materials, so those are covered, but check with your designer to be sure.

Images and Artwork

For stock images, most standard licenses come with a set number of imprints (e.g., copies of your book) that it can be used on. If sales of your book go over that number, then you must purchase an extended license. This is typically a rather large number, so if you exceed it, you can rejoice and be glad you require the extended license. The precise number varies depending on where the image is licensed, so check the fine print wherever you find your image. The responsibility of appropriate licensing falls with you, the author, so make sure your designer is pulling images from a reliable source.

If your image has people in it, then model releases are also required. Reputable stock image sites will note if a model release is on file and what, if any, limitations there are. Again, this is your responsibility. If the use of their image is not according to their contract, you can be sued by the model, and they will most likely win. Ignorance of the law does not excuse you.

Also, beware of any images that include copyrighted or trademarked elements. For example, if someone is dressed as Minnie Mouse and someone takes their photo, the photographer and model may give their consent, but Disney most likely has not. The same would be true of brand names, logos, etc. Again, the burden of the law falls on you as the image is on something you have published. Incidentally, this is true regardless of if the image is on a for-sale product or not. You must adhere to copyright and trademark laws and licensing on your blog as well as on the cover of your book.

Designer

When the designer takes the images, your title, and your author name and compiles them into the cover image for your book, that compilation is by default under their copyright by law. Unless stated otherwise in your contract, you cannot legally change that image in any way or use the image for anything other than its intended purpose. If you need changes, contact the designer, who will make them for you.

The reasons for this are very complex and relate to the use of stock images. This is a gray area, so many reputable designers will err on the side of caution and not give you source files, only finished ones. The artistic reason is that a book's cover design is a carefully crafted piece of art, and undue tinkering will destroy the balance and effectiveness of the design.

Work-for-Hire

Work-for-hire is an exception to the copyright law that the designer or creator owns the copyright to their creation. Work-for-hire can occur in the context of an employee creating work within the scope of their employment. That probably doesn't apply to you, the self-published author. The other exception is when a freelance artist and the client both sign an agreement stating that the work is for hire, and it falls under one of the following nine categories:

- A contribution to a collective work
- A contribution used as part of a motion picture or other audio-visual work
- A supplementary work, which includes pictorial illustrations, maps, and charts, done to supplement a work by another author
- A compilation
- A translation
- An atlas
- A test
- Answer material for a test
- An instructional text (defined as a literary, pictorial, or graphic work prepared for publication and with the purpose of use in systematic instructional activities)

Cover Design

Anything outside of these nine categories cannot be considered work-for-hire with or without a signed contract. [9]

---

9   Artists Guild Graphic, The Graphic Artists Guild Handbook Pricing & Ethical Guidelines, 14th Ed. (New York: Artists Guild Graphic, 2013), 33–34.

A Simple Route to Publishing
Directions for the Journey

Title: _____
Subtitle: _____
Author Name: _____
Imprint: _____
Series & Number: _____
Release Date: _____

ISBNs
eBook: _____   Paperback: _____
Hardback: _____   Audio: _____

Description: _____
_____
_____
_____
_____
_____
_____

Keywords (7): _____
_____
_____

Ebook Categories: _____
_____

Print Categories: _____
_____

Age Range (Children's Books): _____
Trim Size: _____   Paper Color: _____

Ebook Price: _____   Paperback Price: _____
Hardback Price: _____ Audio Price: _____

©2020 Alice Briggs - KingdomCovers.com
Permission granted for copying for personal use only.

CHAPTER EIGHT

Meta Data

ON THE DIRECTIONS for Your Journey Page (p 48) is the metadata that you'll need when you upload your book onto whatever sites you've chosen. The form assumes one pen name and publisher imprint. If you are using an additional imprint or pen name, you might wish to make a note of those.

Metadata is all the behind-the-scenes information that lets the distributors know what kind of book it is and who might be interested in it. Their search engines pay particular attention to the title, subtitle, categories, and keywords. These should be self-explanatory.

Release date is included for future reference and if you are planning a pre-order so you can ensure that date is the same everywhere you upload your book.

ISBN refers to the International Standard Book Number. It is a unique identifier for each format of your book. There is one provider of these per country, and some of you are lucky enough to get them free. Most e-book retailers assign their own numbers, so some people do not use an ISBN for their e-book. Paperback, hardback, and audio will need their own. Both KDP and IS offer free ISBNs, but they belong to those platforms, and it will show them as the publisher of record. It may also confuse libraries and potential readers if they see are two numbers for the same thing. After you've purchased them, you will need to assign an ISBN to each format of your book.

Bowker is the place to purchase ISBNs in the U.S. and Neilson is for the U.K. Canada, France, and South Africa provide them for free for their citizens. Other places selling ISBNs, or giving them away, like KDP and IS have purchased them in bulk, which reduces the price, from the appropriate place in that country and are reselling them.

The description is the sales copy or blurb for your book. This text will sell the book to potential readers once the cover has caught their eye. You can use the Kindlepreneur Book Description Generator[10] to attractively format your description and then paste that into the field at KDP.

Keywords are not just single words but phrases that people might search for to find your book. You have seven available to you in most places.

Categories are where you can drill down to the best niche for your book. Remember the market research you did before? Use that information to help guide your choices here. The categories for print and e-book are slightly different, so this is a great way to increase your discoverability by choosing different but still applicable categories.

If you know what your prices will be, you can make a note of them before you begin. If not, both IS and KDP have suggested prices and/or calculators that show the potential profit at the price points you choose to help you decide. Some people adjust prices for a specific profit per book; others prefer consistent pricing. Again, refer to the research you did earlier to assist you in these choices. Your price is not locked in, so you can adjust this later if you desire.

---

10 https://kindlepreneur.com/amazon-book-description-generator/

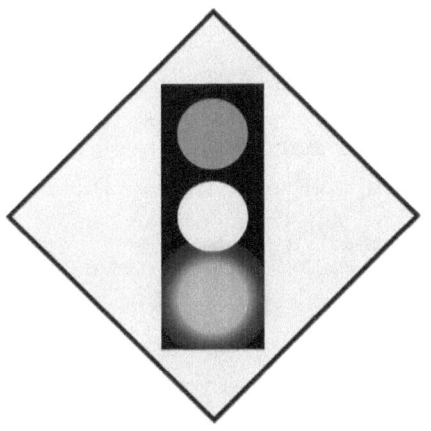

CHAPTER NINE

Publish

YOU WILL NEED to create accounts where you wish to upload your book. I have found this to always be a straightforward process. You will need to have your bank account and tax information handy. That will vary, depending on your legal status as a person or a company, etc., so I can't advise you on specifics. I created most of my accounts a few years ago, so the process may have changed since then. If you become stuck or confused, a search will be helpful.

You will also need to determine what account you wish your royalties deposited into. As far as I know, this must be a checking account at a bank. Some international authors use other services as an intermediary. You can ask in author groups or do an online search to find what works best in your country.

You can do this step whenever you like. If you have time while waiting on editors or cover designers, feel free to get this step out of the way.

Upload

Once you set up your account(s), your book is edited and formatted, your cover is designed, and your metadata is compiled, you are ready to upload your files.

On each platform, you will want to create or add a new title. Each platform requires largely the same information, just not always in the same order.

Some additional questions that you may come across as you upload ask if the book is in the public domain and if you have worldwide rights. If you've written this book and you have not sold or given any rights away, the answer to the first is no and the second is yes. Books in the public domain are those out of copyright (in the US, seventy-five years after the death of the author). In traditional realms, a publisher typically allowed the author to keep the rights to other geographical areas in addition to their primary market.

Your "Directions for the Journey" worksheet will be your guide. Fill in the information as you go along. All platforms have a verification or quality control process that your files will need to go through before the book will be live. I would also recommend purchasing a proof copy of your print books to make sure they look like you think they will. This is also a great time to do a final proofread as your mind will see the book differently in a new form.

When you and the platform are satisfied with your files, you can hit the publish button and then wait for your book to show up on the platform.

If you have published print with KDP and are adding Ingram Spark, speak to a representative for a file transfer. See p. 15 for more.

Royalties

When will you receive the royalties from books sold?

KDP pays sixty days after the end of the month in which the book was sold or the pages read for those in KU.

IS pays ninety days after the book is sold.

Other platforms will have information on the frequency and requirements of their payouts.

When you run ads, remember that you will not see the earnings for a while, but the platforms will want to be paid the same month as you run the ads.

A Simple Route to Publishing
Upload Checksheet

Book Title: _____

Interior:

☐ ePub

☐ mobi

☐ PDF - interior

Cover:

☐ ebook cover

☐ KDP cover

☐ IS cover

Platforms

☐ KDP

☐ IS

☐ Payhip

☐ Website

☐ Kobo

☐ PublishDrive

☐ Smashwords

☐ Streetlib

☐ KDP print (once preorder is live)

CHAPTER TEN

Marketing

CONGRATULATIONS! YOU'VE PUBLISHED your book and completed this leg of your journey! The next leg of that journey is marketing. I am not an expert, and what works depends on so many factors that I can't advise you. I suggest that you look at the 20Booksto50K® Facebook group. Their files contain reams of great information and advice. They are helpful but don't take kindly to people who don't do their own search of the files, as so many questions you'll have are amply answered there.

You will find Facebook groups for nearly any genre of writing that you can think of, so check them out to find helpful people.

IndieAuthorTools.com is a new website with lots of information and tools to use on your journey.

Resources

You can find links to great resources for the rest of your Indie Route Journey at the link below. Enjoy your journey!

https://kingdomcovers.com/indie-route-resources

Author Note

If my counting is correct, I've published or been a contributor to the content of thirty books, including this one. I'm also a designer for book covers and interiors and work with a lot of first-time authors. This book started as a way to answer all the questions that those authors had and that I had myself when I was starting out, so I completely understand. I hope you find it helpful, and that it helps you not become overwhelmed with the process.

I also love to garden, and even though it's January, I'll be starting my tender plants so they'll be ready to put out in the garden once the danger of frost is past. I'll be planting the cold hardy vegetables, such as lettuce, peas, and potatoes, outside. I've only been on this property for a few years, and I'm still figuring out how and what to grow here.

Having a productive garden depends on the sun, the rain—or irrigation here in Texas—the soil, and the seed. For optimal results, all aspects need to be within the preferences for what you're trying to grow. But no matter how perfect the situation is, growing a garden is still a lot of work.

Publishing a book is a lot like that: a lot of factors and a lot of work. But it's all worth it when you hold that final product in your hand.

I hope you persevere through the work and all the many moving parts of the process so that you can continue to move forward until you reap the rewards of your book published.

Enjoy the wonderful adventure of your publishing journey!
Alice

www.ingramcontent.com/pod-product-compliance
Lightning Source LLC
Chambersburg PA
CBHW030201100526
44592CB00009B/382